in defence of adventurous mothers

Simon Marshall

I0141050

methuen | drama

LONDON • NEW YORK • OXFORD • NEW DELHI • SYDNEY

METHUEN DRAMA

Bloomsbury Publishing Plc, 50 Bedford Square, London, WC1B 3DP, UK
Bloomsbury Publishing Inc, 1359 Broadway, New York, NY 10018, USA
Bloomsbury Publishing Ireland, 29 Earlsfort Terrace, Dublin 2,
D02 AY28, Ireland

BLOOMSBURY, METHUEN DRAMA and the Methuen
Drama logo are trademarks of Bloomsbury Publishing Plc.

First published in Great Britain 2025

Artwork by Oli Savage

Bloomsbury Publishing Plc does not have any control over, or responsibility
for, any third-party websites referred to or in this book. All internet addresses
given in this book were correct at the time of going to press. The author and
publisher regret any inconvenience caused if addresses have changed or sites
have ceased to exist, but can accept no responsibility for any such changes.

No rights in incidental music or songs contained in the work are hereby
granted and performance rights for any performance/presentation
whatsoever must be obtained from the respective copyright owners.

All rights whatsoever in this play are strictly reserved and application
for performance etc. should be made before rehearsals begin to the author
via Bloomsbury Publishing, performance.permissions@bloomsbury.com.
No performance may be given unless a licence has been obtained.

A catalogue record for this book is available from the British Library.

Library of Congress Control Number: 2025941208.

ISBN: PB: 978-1-3505-9651-1
ePDF: 978-1-3505-9652-8
eBook: 978-1-3505-9653-5

Series: Modern Plays

Typeset by Mark Heslington Ltd, Scarborough, North Yorkshire

For product safety related questions contact
productsafety@bloomsbury.com.

To find out more about our authors and books visit
www.bloomsbury.com and sign up for our newsletters.

in defence of adventurous mothers

by Simon Marshall

CAST

Nancy	Lucy Wells
Theo	Jack Gray

CREW

Director	Oli Savage
Producer	Eleanor Shaw
Dramaturg	Alice Fitzgerald

With thanks to Derby Theatre and The North Wall Arts Centre

This is a work of fiction. Unless otherwise indicated, all the names, characters, businesses, places, events and incidents in this play are either a product of the writer's imagination or used in a fictitious manner.

This text went to press before the end of rehearsals and so may differ slightly from the play as performed.

"Brims with energy, excitement, and opportunity"
– The Guardian, 2023

VAULT Creative Arts is a multi-award-winning, internationally renowned arts company, and the previous producers of VAULT Festival – London's largest festival of performing arts. We build meaningful, low-risk opportunities for the UK's best emerging talent to grow, develop and make ground-breaking work. We do this by creating exciting, extraordinary cultural events in unexpected locations. We breathe new life into these spaces, filling them with creativity, and inspiring audiences to fill their lives with creativity too.

ᴛʜᴇGLITCH

The Glitch is a vibrant bar/café and unique create space in the heart of Waterloo, created by VAULT Creative Arts. Re-launching in early 2025, the venue has developed a reputation as an intimate, exciting venue for curious audiences to see a range of brilliant comedy, music, cabaret, and special one-off events. The venue combines excellent creative output with exciting social experiences, meaning The Glitch is more than just a performance venue. It's a place to be.

The *VCA Playwriting Award* is a new initiative launched by VAULT Creative Arts. Annually, the company offers an open call for writers to submit scripts for consideration. The winning writer is awarded with a prize fee, and a 4-week production of their script at The Glitch. This is just one of many things VCA does to support and develop early career artists.

in defence of adventurous mothers is the winner of the inaugural VCA Playwriting Award.

Simon Marshall – Writer

Simon Marshall is a playwright, poet and writing facilitator from Derbyshire, living in Sheffield. His writing draws on themes of the rural queer experience, and sense of place, belonging and ambition. He is a former Associate Artist of Derby Theatre, and Associate Poet for Derby Poetry Festival 2024.

His queer coming-of-age audio play *kilburn (not london)* was released on podcast networks everywhere in 2021 and has been heard worldwide, and *BONFIRE*, a solo show exploring the wake of online grooming, had a regional tour in winter 2023. The play was called 'honest, brave and sharply funny' by critic Lyn Gardner, and was called 'an important piece of queer theatre' by reviewers. *Odyssey* a VR Audio Play written with care-experienced group Plus One, went on to win *The Stage* Award for Digital Project of the Year 2023.

Other work includes: *The Fossil Kids* for Sheffield Theatres' Playhouse, June 2023, audio short *Saving Mel Spencer* for Podium. *Me*, April 2025, and *Below Decadence* at Camden People's Theatre, April 2025.

Oli Savage – Director

Oli Savage is an award-winning stage director, and is currently the Artistic Director and CEO of VAULT Creative Arts. He was formerly the co-founder and Artistic Director of The Greenhouse Theatre, the UK's first zero-waste theatre. His shows often involve myth, magic, storytelling and music.

Directing credits with VAULT Creative Arts at The Glitch include: *Sandbox* (2025), *The Lost Library of Leake Street* (2024).

Directing credits with The Greenhouse Theatre include: *To the Ocean* (2023), *Waste Age* (2022, The Design Museum), *As You Like It* (2021), *Swallows* (2019) and *The Voices We Hear* (2019).

Other directing credits include: *Trump L'Oeil* (2022, Upstairs at The Gatehouse), *A Midsummer Night's Dream* (2018, international tour).

Lucy Wells – Nancy

Lucy Wells trained as an actor musician at Rose Bruford College. Since graduating she has worked in various theatre, TV, film and radio roles. She has also worked as a producer for live events, TV and film.

Stage acting credits include: SIRLEY/ SAX, *A Matter of Life and Death* (2025, New Vic Theatre), GOLDILOCKS, *Goldilocks and the Three Bears* (2023, The New Wolsey Theatre), HENNY PENNY, *Henny Penny* (2021, The Garage Norwich), GERDA, *The Snow Queen* (2020, The New Wolsey Theatre), BO PEEP, *Bo Peep* (2020, The Garage Norwich), EMILY PRESTO, *BBC Ten Pieces Live* (2019), Chichester Festival Theatre/UK tour), GENIE, *Aladdin* (2019, The New Wolsey Theatre).

TV/Film credits include: ROBIN, *A Glass House* (2024, Pele Rocket), OFFICE MANAGER, *The Programme* (2024, So Crocodile), AJ, *Champion* (2023, BBC/Netflix), CUSTOMER, *Linda* (2023, My Options Were Limited).

Jack Gray – Theo

Jack is an actor and writer, originally from Leeds. Since graduating from Mountview, Jack has been fortunate enough to have toured the country with a hit show while also appearing in TBA screen projects, as well as writing and starring in an exciting TV pilot that is currently in development.

Theatre credits include: SCUTTLE/ENSEMBLE/MALE UNDERSTUDY, *Unfortunate: The Untold Story of Ursula the Sea Witch* (2022–4) – Southwark Playhouse Elephant and UK tour, JAMES, *Cockfosters* (2023) – Turbine Theatre, ELIAS, *Five Short Plays Loosely Linked by the Theme of Crime* (2022) – Drayton Arms Theatre, KIERAN, *Anti-climax* (2021) – Theatre503, BEN, *Badgers Can't be Friends* (2021) – Southwark Playhouse.

Other credits include: THE CARER, *Glory Be to the Father* (2025) – Short Film, THE WITCH HUNTER, *Death Loves Her Raven* (2024) – Short Film, JOE, *Side Hustle* (2024) – Short Film.

Writer's Note

This play is named after an article by Alison Osius celebrating female mountaineers who not only achieved incredible things in their lifetimes, but faced criticism in the press for doing so while having children, which their male contemporaries did not.

I really hope the play pays tribute to and raises awareness of these women, and the hardship faced in pursuit of following your purpose. I'd recommend researching mountaineers such as Hilaree Nelson, Alison Hargreaves, Chantal Mauduit, Catherine Destivelle and Liliane Barrard to get a sense of the scale of their achievement and dedication.

I've always found my mum's friendship with Alison Hargreaves very inspiring, and what it's meant to follow your passions wholeheartedly. Mum would talk about them climbing together in the Peak District as teenagers, and male climbers stopping to ask if they needed any help, because it was so unusual to see two young women on the rocks by themselves.

Personally, Mum making her career change in 2017, returning to her love of the outdoors and becoming one of the few female mountain leaders in the UK, coincided with when I started pursuing writing seriously.

Her committing to and persevering with her goals feels like maybe the best thing you can do as a parent, which is to give your children permission to try, and to keep going.

That coloured a lot of what went into this play too, alongside how you build back from tragedy, what you use your time on Earth for, and what makes a legacy. So I owe Mum a lot. Cheers, Bev.

I've been fortunate enough to have had some incredible female mentors and collaborators along the way to writing this, who've taught me the ropes in many other ways too, and who I want to thank:

Jane Upton, who dared me to write about what I'm scared of.

Sam Potter, for being the first person to talk to me like I was a proper playwright, and who reminded me it was a play about love!

Lucy Haighton, for getting me moving, thinking and feeling my way through this play.

Alice Fitzgerald, for her friendship, encouragement and incredible dramaturgical eye.

Helen Dobson, for her kindness and support (and thanks to you and Will for taking me climbing!).

Nicky Bellenger for being such an incredible champion of me early on, and Derby Theatre with Sarah Brigham at the helm for your immense support of me always.

A huge thank you to the North Wall Arts Centre and their Catalyst programme in 2023 where I first got to share 'in defence', and the incredible artists and friends I got to work alongside. Urgh, love you. Special mentions to Ria Parry, Tom Brennan, Karim Khan, Dale Edwards, Layla Chowdhury, Robyn Sinclair, Rori Hawthorn and Lizzie Twells for their voices contributing to this play along the way, and huge love to Andy Owens for his immense generosity on this project throughout.

Thanks to Omnibus Theatre for including us at Next Page in January 2025, and that first wonderful audience too.

And to all the Liam Mullinses, past and future. Great arms. Cheers all.

In pushing this play (and me!) up the hill, I send huge love to Hope and Laura, Grace and Ellie, Mitchell and Andrew, Alice, Katherine, Rio and Callan, and Sian and the team at Methuen Drama for being so lovely.

Oli and Ellie for believing in 'in defence' and awarding it the first VCA Playwriting Award, thank you hugely, and to Jack and Lucy for being the first to step into the roles of Theo and Nancy officially. Am so excited to set off with you all.

Finally, to Dad, Joe and Grandpa, thanks for being there every step of the way.

And back to Mum. You're a rockstar. Get your walking boots on.

Adventure awaits!

Loadsa love

Simon x

A portion of proceeds from this play text will be donated to Himalayan Rescue Association Nepal, who seek to reduce casualties on mountains in the Nepal Himalayas.

in defence of adventurous mothers

For Mum

Characters

Theo, *32, increasingly risk-averse, earthbound.*

Nancy, *28, increasingly intrepid, cloudbound.*

This is a play for two performers, with other characters shared between them both, except Mum's voice, which should be pre-recorded. The play is active, and should be embodied in its performance, perhaps climbing ropes, climbing set, climbing over each other in the telling of it.

Content warning: contains themes of grief and parent loss.

Scene One

Theo *and* **Nancy** *as children sat on a stone ledge together in the Peak District.*

Theo   Where does the mountain begin then?

If it's soil and rock and ice and snow and beetles and flowers and clouds and wind and people.

Where does it begin?

Nancy   Under your feet!

That's where it is.

Obviously.

Theo   Alright! Well, where does it end then, smart arse?

Nancy   Well there'll be a next one and a next one and a next one and a next one.

Shout with me.

Shout with me so Mum can hear us.

Theo   What are we shouting?

Nancy   We need to tell her we love her.

Theo   *No, we don't.*

Nancy   We need to tell her we love her or she won't come back.

Theo   That's not true.

Nancy   How do you know?

How do you know?

Theo   I'm not doing that.

Scene Two

As Mum's voice is heard, **Theo** *and* **Nancy** *move and play and climb under and over each other. They seem to grow up as the entry continues.*

Mum's Voice   The mountain's under my feet.

The peaks of my toes, these Roman toes, line up perfectly with Annapurna 1.

I am sat by a stream, with edelweiss and a pink flower I do not recall the name of.

And I miss you both dreadfully, Theo and Nancy. My world is quieter without you. It's enough to make me pack up and come back on the next rickety van down the valley.

The papers would never let me hear the end of it.

But I know you're safe with your dad. Thank you, Richard. Thank you for holding them when I can't. And me when I just want to roam.

I hope you know I'm safe here. The peaks are my friends, they know what I need and what's good for me.

Our season to do the ascent is short, and so much of climbing is weather watching and reading the future. But not looking down. Never looking down.

I can't cry when I climb because the moisture will freeze fast, but a smile warms my breath.

Thank you for making me smile.

Sweet Nancy with your eyes wide as sunsets and your smile Theo could hang onto like a monkey.

The moon's up and out like a carabiner I can count on, when the sky's this clear.

I leave tonight. And I won't be long my dears.

With any luck I'll be back by September.

Theo *and* **Nancy** *stop playing.*

Scene Three

Nancy *alone.* **Theo** *upstairs.*

Nancy   The months after, we'd be very still.

She looks over at **Theo.** *Nothing . . .*

After the *main* sadness.

Getting picked up early from a school trip to Twycross Zoo. And the press.

Lots of holding Dad's hands. And not looking up.

Theo   Expecting her in crowds.

Nancy   I can remember lots of evenings of Dad and I just sitting very still together.

Us in the lounge by a timid fire, surrounded by climbing books and adventure guides and framed pictures of the Alps and the Himalayas and just being sat together dormant.

Theo two floors up again in the attic.

Not coming down.

We must've ate dinner and we must've said some things, but the overwhelming feeling was silence.

I'd come upstairs and wrap leftover spaghetti in paper and try and slide it through his door frame.

Dad didn't love that.

But he'll have been hungry.

Theo   We were half living.

'Her poor kids.' The papers said.

I'd come downstairs in the night to eat Rice Krispies and read the headlines.

Circle words like 'abandoned', 'devastated', 'selfish'.

Keep the papers. This reporter Sam Randall weighing in about how our family would be ruined forever now. Those poor kids. Because of what Mum did.

We were her poor kids.

Nancy   *And* Dad's.

And I did try to involve Theo.

'Theo, where do you think Snap, Crackle and Pop live?'

Theo (as Dad)   'Theo, have your dinner please before Nancy tries to fit it through the bloody keyhole.'

Nancy   'Theo, do you bring your passport with you when you climb up to heaven?'

Theo   Dad would smile at me all the time like 'how you doing champ, how you doing bud, how you doing kid, how you doing lad?'.

Nancy   He'd smile to show he didn't have any answers.

Theo   He didn't have a clue anymore.

Nancy   He'd smile when he dropped us off at the school gates.

Theo   'The poor bloke.'

Or when we'd ask why we were no longer invited to MegaZone, or Rollerworld or Paint a Pot parties.

Nancy   'They can't catch sadness, can they Daddy?'

I think he smiled like he wished he could help.

Theo   He'd smile fucking helplessly.

And say he was tired and 'heading up the wooden hill to Bedfordshire.'

Nancy   'But we're in Derbyshire, that's ages away.'

And he'd thud thud thud away.

Theo   And Nancy's footsteps after him like a little goat. Like a little bleating goat.

Nancy   'What's in Bedfordshire anyway? Is Mum in Bedfordshire?'

Sometimes he would stop and just put his hand on my chin like he was cupping a snow globe.

And I'd only cry then.

Theo   I was twelve and Nancy was eight when Mum didn't come back.

I was so tired. All the time. Too tired to laugh, or run like she would.

To have energy. So so much energy.

Nancy always got there quicker.

Nancy   It was a birthday party.

I got to secondary school, and although teachers knew who we were and some parents must have started to clock from my name, the kids in my class didn't.

So I was just Nancy. And she was just Lisa Radecki.

Asking if I wanted to come on Saturday 24th, 'it's all here on this', handing me a paper invite with a clipart border and *RSVP!* in bubble writing. Did I want to come to her twelfth Birthday Party?

It's at 'Wild Walls which is next to Matalan which is next to the cinema.'

'Do you want to come climbing with us?'

. . . And I did. I really did.

Scene Four

Lisa's birthday party. **Nancy** *looking up at the wall to climb ahead of them.*

Robert Bollington   Come on, Nancy!

It's your go, there's no point just standing at the bottom looking at it.

You should be really good at this.

That's what my dad said. He said 'watch out for that Nancy she'll be really good at this because it'll be in her blood.'

Is it in your blood?

And what is 'it' do you think? That my dad was talking about?

Is it 'onomatopoeia'? Mrs Sampson's always talking about that. Is that what that is?

Nancy.

Is it onomatopoeia in your blood?

Nancy (*to audience*)   It was actually quite high.

You imagine the climbing wall to have to be child-friendly, but even on the bouldering wall the top felt like a long way up. Like a cheese grater or a mouth with lots of coloured fillings. Snarling at us.

Robert Bollington   Nancy, if you're too scared can I go in front please?

Nancy (*scared*)   Rob, shut up I'm concentrATING.

I gave him a thump on the arm.

I remember Mum used to say that all the best things in life happen in orange. Not red for danger, not amber to pause, but the orange in between, of sunsets and energy and my little plastic climbing helmet, at Wild Walls next to Matalan next to the cinema.

So I put my hands on the coloured grooves in the wall, and sprang up. It made sense, it made sense, like a playground. Or a puzzle just –

Robert Bollington   – Err, you're not allowed to touch ones of a different colour actually Nancy.

Nancy (*shouting down at him*)   BUT it's QUICKER this way.

But then I'd looked down and it had become something else.

Really quite high. My ears went a bit funny. And Rob's voice was muffled by the tinny pop music playing. And my blood in my ears.

And there's only one supervising parent and he's nursing a vending machine mocha half the building away.

It's getting embarrassing and not just embarrassing, a little bit worrying.

Robert Bollington   She's not gonna do it, Lisa. She's gonna stay up there forever. She's too scared I think.

Nancy   Lisa's starting to ask her dad if they can get me down. 'I don't think she likes it.'

The crew are scrambling in their satsuma-coloured fleeces.

(*To herself.*) Come on, Nancy.

And then.

A familiar piano key. Like the blood in my pulse settling into a rhythm, a determination.

Perhaps an instrumental of 'The Climb' by Miley Cyrus begins to play gently in the background.

And I actually CAN *almost see it.*

But there's a voice getting in the way.

Robert Bollington   You'll never reach it!

Nancy   Shut up Robert Bollington.

And my body starts to read the wall a bit.

Like it knows the story after all. Like I just had my eyes closed up until now.

Half asleep.

I tense like a spring.

Or a rocket.

Give my hands and feet the signal.

And I launch.

LIFT OFF, all the way to the top.

When I've touched the top, I drop down, and land on the sprung floor like a –

I'd love to say it was Mum's voice which rallied me on.

But it wasn't.

It wasn't even Miley Cyrus'.

It was mine.

Scene Five

Nancy *pulls out better kit from her bag and gets changed into more heavy-duty climbing gear.* **Theo** *joins her.*

Nancy   And then I got serious.

Properly serious.

Theo and I would go to the climbing wall Tuesdays, Thursdays and Saturdays.

Theo   Well it made sense childcare-wise, for Dad.

He didn't come along at first.

I was wary too.

Nancy   Theo took to it really naturally.

Theo   No, I was always a bit wary.

Nancy   But you were gnarly like a spider with a puberty tash.

Theo   And she was small and fast like a lynx or some kind of wall-rat.

Nancy   Theo that's not nice, is it? Wall-rat.

It just felt amazing to be good at something. Really naturally good at something.

Theo   And it did calm something in me, I suppose.

When you're growth-spurting and it feels like your hormones are pushing at every available surface. To have something that was still and certain, and conquerable.

Nancy   And to get to do it together.

Theo   And spot each other.

Nancy   And look back at Dad, and see him smiling. But meaning it this time.

Theo (*as* **Dad**)   'Go on, Nance!'

Nancy   We were the climbing staff's favourites, because we learned fast and asked good questions –

Theo   and let them use us on their flyers.

Nancy   We'd get free hot chocolates.

And Dad would help them plot new problems and routes.

And they'd tell him;

'That lad of yours is a credit to you.'

(*To* **Theo**.) They did, Theo.

Theo   Well mainly they were saying:

Nancy   'She's becoming the spit of her Mum, isn't she?'

Scene Six

Theo's *bedroom*.

Theo   I don't know what your mum is meant to be for you when you're a teenager.

Like there's a lot of things I'm glad she didn't walk in on.

And I wasn't the hugging type, try as Nancy might. But when I started buying climbing magazines.

And looking at the men and women in their harnesses.

And the arses of the men in their harnesses.

And like avoiding certain instructors at Wild Walls because they had jawlines like cut marble and the straps of the harness would, erm, bulge just so.

I couldn't tell Mum. Obviously.

Nancy was on another planet.

But there's this guy who would come and spot me and Nancy when we were on new problems. He went to Atterbury College which is the other village away from us.

And he was. Yeah, he was alright-looking I suppose.

Great arms. Just. Yeah. Liam Mullins.

But given I was thinking all that. Quite urgently. And he'd come over after I'd done one of the experienced routes and give me a hug 'well done!'

And I would m e l t.

I could be the hugging type for him.

So when I did tell Dad, age sixteen.

'Dad, I think I. I might like boys like you're meant to like girls.'

And it was silence again. And no smile.

Theo *looks at a wall to climb ahead of him.*

So the next day in between fourth and fifth period I climbed to the roof of the school.

I couldn't breathe at ground level. Double Maths, IT, I was shut tight like a bear trap, seething through it. It felt like my vision was narrowing.

So on the way from the Humanities Block to Media. I saw the little Quiet Area sign. Bright orange.

And really fancied that. My own peace. And a problem to solve.

And how the route would be bench, drainpipe, cornicing, disabled loo roof, dining hall roof. Summit.

And did it.

Grazed my school trousers, cut my hands on the guttering, worried about tetanus as it throbbed and throbbed, but.

Forget Miley Cyrus. I was Evanescence.

Waking up inside. *Can't wake up.*

My breath settling again after the effort, but then peace.

The view. The field down to the brook. Our little village. Our house. The farms with their cows sort of blundering about.

There's no space for words up here.

True quiet.

I mean when the bell then went it was fucking loud.

And the whistles started blowing.

Nancy   When Mr Entwistle came to the door to tell Mrs Sampson.

Mr Entwistle   Can Nancy collect her things and come with me please?

Nancy   My heart fell through my feet screaming 'not good, not good, not good, not good'.

I wouldn't budge.

Mr Entwistle   You've not done anything wrong Nancy.

Listen Nancy, come with me, you're not in trouble.

Your Nana's at reception alright?

Your Dad's with your brother. There's been an incident.

NO, no. They'll be fine. Hey, he'll be fine I'm sure.

Nancy   Nana made rock cakes and tried to distract me but 'not good not good not good not good'.

Theo   Calling the Fire Service was overkill I think.

But apparently the caretaker's ladders weren't long enough because –

Nancy (*as* **Caretaker**)   'We never need to go that high Maureen, roofers have their own.

Blurryell. We don't want to spook him like a sodding cat, do we?'

Theo   I had 10 minutes until they arrived. Coming down was going to be harder work than I might have first thought, to be fair.

Not just because of the kids pouring out their classes, cus, if you knew weird Theo was on the roof you'd be distracted from *Of Mice and Men* as well.

I couldn't find the route down so easy, because your perception's skewed when you're looking down.

And also I didn't *want* to go.

So I sat tight, until Dad appeared.

Giving him a megaphone made everything feel a bit camp and like a protest chant.

Nancy (*as* **Dad**)   Come down!

Theo   No thanks!

Nancy (*as* **Dad**)   . . . What do you want?

Theo   Some time.

Nancy (*as* **Dad**)   When do you want it?

Theo   Now.

(*To audience.*) And the Deputy Head told him off for 'trying to negotiate with terrorists'.

Nancy (as Dad)   This is very serious, Theodore.

If you come down now.

You'll be in slightly less trouble than you already are.

But you *are* grounded.

Theo   How?

Nancy (*as* **Dad**; *off megaphone*)   Cheeky git.

(*Back on megaphone.*) Listen.

I just want you to be safe, Theo.

Do what you like, live how you like.

I just want you and your sister to be safe.

I don't care if you're gay.

I don't!

Sorry, I mean, if you're as you say you are. I didn't mean you to feel ashamed.

I just want you to be safe. And happy.

Theo   So that's how Dad accidentally outed me to the whole school. As a broadcast.

It took three firemen to get me down.

He smiles.

Best Wednesday ever.

AND.

Liam texted that night to say he'd seen me on the news and thought what I'd done was 'pretty hardcore'.

Best Wednesday ever ever.

Scene Seven

Nancy   The press had a field day.

'Like Mother Like Son!'

'Ill-fated mountaineer Rita Debenham's eldest child holds up school day with risky move to climb Fincham Community School's original antique roof.

His mother famously disappeared on Annapurna 1 –'

Theo   Fucking Sam Randall.

Nancy   'His father, pictured here, desperate to bring his son back to safety.

It's unclear of the so-called "Roof Boy's motivations".'

Attention, obviously.

He did a little victory lap at Wild Walls and everyone complimented his technical skill and how ungrippy school shoes are.

He didn't even climb that night.

May as well have not bothered coming.

Liam had a moped so they'd often do a stupid little drive around the block to get ice cream whilst I climbed. I dunno, something like that.

Theo   It was gelato actually.

Heavenly Desserts.

I was suspended for a week and then got reintroduced into the timetable gradually like an endangered species.

'Roofboy' didn't last long. When people in my year started the rumour that I slept up there, it became 'Batboy' and then 'Batty'.

Genius.

By the time I got to sixth form I was still working at the centre but barely touched the wall myself. Just watched.

Nancy   Liam bought him a locket for his seventeenth birthday.

It was hideous.

Theo   I really like it.

Nancy   It was hideous.

Liam also started picking Theo up from home when he'd passed his driving test.

Dad'd wave them off.

Theo (*as* **Dad**)   Mind how you go lads.

Nancy   I started doing a lot more solo climbing the years after that.

And watched the definition in my shoulders change. I don't know if puberty was kind or just my body felt purpose purpose purpose because when I was seventeen I was lean and nimble. I was in peak physical condition.

Trekking out to the peaks most evenings. Bloodied knuckles on 'Black Car Burning' and stretches of edges I was closer to than any friend.

Weekends in Wales staying at youth hostels when I could.

Improving my technique. And you make friends but it's circumstantial, it was all about the place for me.

Dream up summer trips to Fontainebleau in France and the Dolomites in Italy.

Nights that I'd rock in after dark because I'd climbed out at the Edges above Hathersage until the sun set and Dad would say

Theo (*as* **Dad**)   'Wondered if you were coming back.

Nancy. You been alright? I've barely seen you in days.

Look at your hands. Jesus are you chalking at all?

There's lasagne in the oven but by now it's probably grown hooves and walked off again.'

Nancy   Cheers.

Theo (*as* **Dad**)   Do you not want a plate? Surprised you're even using a fork.

Nancy, will you look at me please?

Your brother's missed you.

I say your brother's missed you.

Nancy   Has he? Where is he then?

Theo (*as* **Dad**)   Attic.

Go find him will you?

Nancy   And I'd lug myself up the stairs, muscles aching, longing for bed and there he'd be on his PlayStation hunched over like a troll thing. Digits flexing around a controller as I rub my callouses.

Theo   Ey up.

Nancy   Gollum with acne.

Theo   You do alright then?

Nancy   And I'd describe the footholds left by hundreds before us, this language left in the rock for us to read. And how other female climbers look at each other with this special sense of camaraderie. That it's how I imagine troops feel.

And he'd turn the sound up on *Call of Duty*.

'How can you sit around and just do this?

Did you not want to come with?

Theo, did you not want to come with?'

Theo   That's a double negative, did I not want to come with.

Need to learn you some school, Nance.

Nancy   Fine. Leave you to your zombies. You're such a melt.

Theo   I don't bounce like you do.

If I fell now it'd really hurt. Would have to take time off work, it's not practical Nancy.

Nancy   You were good though.

Just need to improve your technique.

A little less gelato maybe, tone up again.

Theo   What the fuck?

Nancy   Tomorrow, Curbar Edge. Belay with me at least. Spot me.

Theo   Yeah I'll spot you disappearing over the edges.

Nancy   Come with me then.

Theo   Nancy, if you get serious, and you start looking at universities.

Yaknow, Sheffield has tonnes of walls nearby.

Nancy   I don't need walls, Theo.

Where we're going, we don't need walls.

Theo   You're embarrassing.

Nancy   *You're embarrassing.* What are you doing with your potential?

Just spaffing it away.

Theo   Nance.

Nancy   I mean it. You could be good, you're at the centre all the time, and you're not even training.

Spending all your time with Liam, yaknow he's not even technically that good. He's a lazy climber. Doesn't move his hips at all.

Theo   We've got plans that aren't climbing.

Nancy   He's a drag.

You're a drag.

I hear you at the wall, your priorities are way off.

Insisting they get a proper coffee machine, what do you want to be a barista for?

Theo   It's a good side job for uni. Manchester's got to be full of cafes.

Nancy   URGH. It's so boring.

You expect so little from yourself.

Theo   Alright, this isn't a TED Talk.

What about actual practical life stuff? When are you gonna climb a fucking UCAS application Nance?

You're literally seventeen, who do you think you are?

You need to get a bit real.

Nancy (*to audience*)   Dad could hear us arguing and hollered up.

Theo (*as* **Dad**)   Y'alright up there?

Kids?

Nancy   I'm not a child!

Theo   You're not God's gift to climbing either.

You think you're carving your own route, but it's all been done, Nancy.

You're always gonna be Mum's kid and you're not even great like she was.

Nancy   Fuck off.

Theo (*as* **Dad**)   What's going on in here, like bloody scrapping cats both of you.

Nancy   I'm better than Mum was! She would want us to do something brilliant.

Nancy (*as* **Dad**)   Ah, you're not better than your Mum, Nancy.

Nance, listen here.

You know, I know that you've really found something that you're passionate about.

And that is lovely to witness.

But I can't let that be all you do. You're not good enough to just do this.

You're gonna want a degree.

Geography?

Or can be something practical.

An apprenticeship.

Theo   You're not even listening.

Are you yawning?

Nancy   How long have you two been thinking this then?

Just said nothing.

Have you always both been this fucking. Mediocre.

If you actually knew Mum.

If you actually wanted to do right by her, you'd be out doing something.

It's like you don't love her enough.

Or me.

And you didn't love her enough to make staying here worth it either.

Theo (*as* **Dad**)   That was out of order Nancy.

Go on, go to bed.

I don't want to see you.

Scene Eight

Theo   And she hardened then.

Got meaner. Turned down lifts from Dad.

Wasn't invited to parties.

Withheld smiles at Christmas.

Just tough tough tough, keeping her own rhythms, in and of the house.

Got a job at a big outdoors retailer.

I won't say which one but they were dickheads. But she got a discount and she started building a weaponry of equipment in her bedroom.

When I'd come home from uni you'd see her trail through the house but never quite catch her. Like a twister or a wildcat.

Carabiners, ropes, buckles, harnesses, shoes, kit bags –

Nancy   'Food: we've got dehydrated, just add heat, energy gels, hydration supplements. At some point on a mountain you stop expecting to eat solids. Everything becomes pastes, bars and mush.

But you'll like them! Promise.'

And I started to hear about trips from customers.

'Oh we're heading out to the Cairngorms tomorrow morning.'

'You haven't ice climbed yet? I can show you.'

Some of these guys would be five, ten, fifteen years older than me.

But when you're packed in the backseat of some estate car, hearing about treks they did with crisp Alpine air and rock faces sheer and tall as gods and you realise these are people that are making their time count. The greats just walking amongst us. In RAB jackets.

Some mention Mum which is.

Yeah, it's nice.

And they ask how I feel working at

Theo   Dickhead's.

Nancy   And you can tell they're thinking.

'Ahh it's great she's interested but she'll never yaknow. Properly do it. Make it.

She's not great like her Mum.'

It comes over me like a wind up my skin. As we go 80mph in a worn-out Corsa up the motorway.

'I actually plan to do all the 8,000 metres my mum did.

And Annapurna 1. *And come down again.*'

The car goes silent like the moment before a rocket launch.

And then Grant Matthews, this proper seasoned mountain type, chunters:

'Well you're going to need press aren't you?

Some backing. If you want to be sponsored. Brand partnerships.

It's a buyers' market, Nance.

But I might know someone.'

Scene Nine

Theo   I'm sat in my first lecture.

Looking at myself on the screen in front of me, blown up in epic proportions.

My little eight-year-old eyes in a charming onesie. Nancy cuddled against Mum's arm like one of those types of shellfish with suction cups.

My stomach has dropped 3 floors below.

Lecturer   *'Sam Randall's coverage of Rita Debenham's career and disappearance is a perfect example of the impact of tabloid journalism on the public's perception of tragedy.*

Before her last expedition, for example, she's quoted in the few interviews she did agree to, as saying that "I simply wouldn't climb if I didn't intend to come down again. I'm not irresponsible."

Oh there's time for questions at the end.'

Theo *realises his hand is in the air. He begins to speak.*

Errm Rita Debenham was fearless so.

So I don't think she would have been fazed. I don't think she would have wanted to be treated any easier because she was our – a mum.

Lecturer   *Well it's not really a question of being treated easier. Some people feel she was treated more than fairly. Given the consequences of her actions.*

As you can see on the next slide –

Theo   Oh.

(*To audience.*) And there I am in a little suit. A picture snapped in the cemetery.

And I'm broken there. Holding Nancy's stupid little hand.

With a headline above saying 'World-famous, World-crushed.'

They shouldn't have taken pictures there. That's private.

Lecturer   Not that it's especially relevant but Richard, the father, gave consent for this particular article.

Theo   Dad did?

Lecturer   Can I ask you to sit down please?

Is it Theo?

Shall we take a break there?

Nancy, *three years later at a climbing conference.*

Nancy   I'm happy to take some questions.

Reporter   Nancy, how ready do you feel?

Nancy   Oh, it's in my blood! I've been prepping for this since I was climbing the wooden hill to Bedfordshire.

The reporter laughs, she laughs too.

They loved that.

I've had a great season in the Alps: The Matterhorn in 5 hours.

Dolomites. Mont Blanc.

But seriously, I have incredible peers, mentors and obviously some big footsteps to fill.

And for a moment I think I've got it right. And then.

Reporter   Your mother was called a once-in-a-generation athlete.

Do you feel lightning can really strike twice in the same family?

Nancy   The less lightning at these heights the better!

I've worked very hard. Am working very hard.

And learning from those that went before me.

We all owe each other, don't we? You're never really climbing alone.

Reporter   So you won't make your mother's mistakes?

Nancy   A ripple amongst the crowd there.

Mum didn't make mistakes. She was careful.

Reporter   With respect. The collective professional opinion is that she was headstrong and not receptive to advice.

Nancy   I'm not here to talk about Mum.

Reporter   Do you not climb because your mum did though?

Nancy   No. I climb because I'm meant to be a climber. Are you rude because your mum was?

Reporter   Why risk it, Nancy?

Nancy   I think we're done for today.

Nancy *settles like she's down from a podium. She reels and then.*

Wait.

Theo?

What are you doing here?

Theo   – It's a placement.

Nancy   Do you want to get a drink or –?

Theo   I'm only passing through really.

You alright?

Nancy   That was murder.

Why didn't you say anything?

Theo   Didn't want to take your thunder.

They asked my question anyway.

Nancy   What was yours?

Theo   Why risk it, Nancy?

Nancy   Oh right.

It's not about risk it's about skill and expertise and effort, actually.

And I've got all that.

Did you not see the Peak-Kit promo? I've got good backers.

Theo   Your new jackets.

Nancy   I'm doing it right, I'm not just throwing myself at the first thing that comes my way.

What I'm doing has integrity.

Actually. I think I'm doing something properly worthwhile.

Theo   Unlike journalism?

Nancy   I mean.

It's beneath you.

Theo   Alright, I'm sure you think so.

Nancy   Yep.

The hyenas won't turn on you if you're one of them, is that it?

Theo   You do know it's a lot of work, Nancy. What you're setting off to do.

I don't know if you read Mum's diaries.

But she put in some hours.

Nancy   I've *been* trying. Haven't I?

You read Mum's diaries?

When?

Theo   Dad has them.

Nancy   And he reads them too?

Why?

Theo   Because they're all he has of her.

Nancy   Oh nice one.

Theo   Will you go see him whilst you're in the area?

Come back to the flat for dinner with me and Liam?

You won't.

Nancy   I'm trying to only be around people who are rooting for me.

Theo   Enablers?

Grant Matthews. God, he's bad news yaknow.

If you'd done . . . any research.

There's a reason he only backs young women, right.

Nancy   Because enough men have had the spotlight and it's important we diversify the pool of –

Theo   Because all his male contemporaries can't fucking stand him.

Nancy   Alright Theo, this has been really special.

I'll leave you to it.

Theo   And you won't be calling Dad?

Even letting him know you're setting off anywhere?

Because if you don't the only way he'll even know –

Is when I write about it.

. . . (*He stands feeling proud of himself for a moment. And then to himself.*) – the fuck's the exit . . .?

Scene Ten

Nancy (*as* **Dad**)   She's her mother's daughter, Theo.

Theo   But I believe we get to *choose* our paths, and at the moment she's choosing to be a dic –

Nancy (*as* **Dad**)   – A different route.

Much like her mother, actually.

Theo   Well she can't *be* Mum.

Nancy (*as* **Dad**)   No, she can't.

Theo   And does she call you?

Nancy (*as* **Dad**)   No.

Theo   – and that doesn't –?

Nancy (*as* **Dad**)   She writes. She does write.

Theo   What does she write?

Nancy (*as* **Dad**)   Emails. Postcards.

Theo   How generous of her.

Nancy (*as* **Dad**)   She had some things to say about her coverage in the *Daily Beacon*, that's for sure.

Are you done?

You said *you* had news?

Theo   Yes. Yes.

Nancy (*as* **Dad**)   What is it then, work?

Theo   Errm.

A year-long position actually.

At . . . the *Daily Beacon*.

Nancy (*as* **Dad**)   That's a –

That's a choice you've chosen isn't it.

Theo It's gonna be very good for me.

Career wise, progression, exposure, escalation.

Nancy (*as* **Dad**) *I'm sure.*

Right.

I've got *some cuttings from them, my lad.*

No doubt about that.

Sam Randall's finest.

If you want them. To brush up.

And you enjoy it? Journalism.

Theo Helps me make sense of things. I think. Follow the trail.

Nancy (*as* **Dad**) Mhmm. Best make a good impression won't you.

. . .

Will you be staying for your dinner?

Theo You don't need to be passive aggressive.

If you're disappointed.

You can just say.

(*To* **Nancy**.) And what he said was.

'In my position, I have found.

I don't get to be passive aggressive do I.

Or aggressive. Especially.

Because then I'd run the risk of being seen as "difficult".

And seeing. Seeing even less of you. You both.

So I just get passive, don't I? That's my option. Always has been.

But I will never have it said, I've not supported you.

Actively. Both of you. All three of you, actually.

Never. You try making your mum see reason, it was like negotiating with a hurricane.

And I know we've had our. Our complications. Theo.

But.

I have tried haven't I?

Being a father to you. When I met you. Three years old and shy and all elbows and knuckles. You took some winning over. But you made having Nancy the easiest thing. Because you showed me how much . . . I had in me.

Of all my pursuits. I have meant this one. As much as I can.

As wholeheartedly as I have in me.

Because you both stagger me. With what ambition you have. What you've made from so little.

So who am I against that . . . force, too.

Might as well join you.'

Nancy   Dad said that?

Theo   Yep.

It's what made me want to be one too, I think.

. . .

Shall we do a fun bit now?

Nancy   Fiinnnne.

So from what you've told me.

Next for Theo was well.

You and Liam getting *serious*.

Chronic.

City mini-breaks and inviting friends for New Year's.

Joint accounts.

You know when couples start only buying one present for birthdays.

'From us both.'

The one organism.

Amoeba.

Theo   And what would you get us?

Exactly.

And then.

On one such mini break. Stockholm.

He.

(*To* **Nancy**.) and if you're being him can you please do it nicely?

Nancy   Sure.

(*As* **Liam**.) Theodore.

I think.

What I think is. Awh I'm not great at speeches.

We've had these past 10 years together. Haven't we?

And that's. That's a long time. And I've been thinking.

Theo   Are you breaking up with me in Stockholm? In front of this Abba Museum?

Nancy (*as* **Liam**)   No, but knowing me.

Knowing you.

Has been just. My most favourite thing I've ever done. Could think of doing.

And I. Just want more of that.

As much of that.

As you'll give me. Please. Thanks.

If you want to? Too?

Like in a marriage way.

Theo   And I did.

I do.

Nancy (*as* **Liam**)   Sound.

Nancy   And then it's engagement messages.

And a party to plan.

And I can hear it in his voicemails.

Theo   Oh so you did listen to them.

Nancy   Hear him disappearing into this idolised future of his.

Theo   Right. Meanwhile.

You're what? A party girl?

Nancy   Well that's what the papers said.

Over après club music.

The thing that the museums and articles and books and outdoor clothing shops don't do justice to is how fucking FUN it gets, too.

When risks are high and your time on trips is SHORT, the nights are exceptional.

You feel alcohol quicker at altitude and climbing boots are more sturdy than heels at least.

Great for climbing on tables.

And I'd get called

Trouble.

And *a right one, that one.*

And my favourite.

Bad news.

Because, how can I be bad news when the outlook's this good?

Music subsides.

Theo   And she started dropping boyfriends like books.

Nancy   And girlfriends.

Theo   The girls that would hang out with you.

That didn't think you were an embarrassment. That weren't making digs at you across panel events at mountaineering festivals.

And in your articles you say

Nancy   *'It's a team sport. Above all else.*

You've got to use the available resources however best you can.

Body heat.

Expeditions ahead of you, behind.'

And this way I was able to hitch a ride on trips from the Alps, to the Andes, to *the Himalayas.*

Grant Matthews going on radio shows saying I'm the most promising thing happening to British climbing. Since. Since Mum.

And when you're actually living your potential.

It can't help but feel like she's. Close.

Scene Eleven

Theo   Liam did warn me.

That yes, yes absolutely 'you invite her.

And if there's a role, a something she could do. Something you know, on the edges.

But.

But a speech, Theo?'

I thought that's the only way she might go along with it to be honest.

Is if she knew she had something to do.

And got some of the attention as well.

And I'd sat her at a table by a fire exit anyway.

If she needed to bolt.

But I was already leaving an empty chair for Mum.

So, just practically.

I wanted every other seat filling.

And Nancy RSVP'd. Yes. I'll be there. *S'il vous plait*.

You did *s'il vous plai*t.

Nancy   I had been invited on an expedition to Lhotse. Which is.

Hoo.

It's Everest's shoulder effectively. Its little sister.

It's 8,516 metres above sea level, which is. Extraordinary.

And Grant Matthews has assembled this team; Canada, UK, France.

Chantal Mauduit became the first woman to ascend it in 1996. She was French. And she was deeply fabulous.

And if I did it.

I would be one of the first five British women to ever.

And it would be my first 8,000+ metre mountain.

Make my name.

Mum never did this one. Never attempted it. And Grant Matthews only chooses the best.

Theo   It was an exciting time for both of us.

Dad and I would check in each week and talk through how I was feeling and the catering and photography and also how your trip was looking.

You were due back before the wedding so. So there was no reason not to be there.

Nancy   Altitude affects everyone differently, and your aptitude to it . . .

Particularly, at 8,000 metres and above is the difference between navigating life and death.

Supplementary oxygen, these tanks that you'd carry to help combat the thinner air.

Well it can be regarded as reducing the achievement. Turning your 8,000-metre mountain into a 6,000-metre one.

Taking the shine off it somewhat.

So we agreed, as a team, that we wouldn't be using them.

We'd have the tanks with us in case of emergency.

But the brief was to just do it. Brave it.

Theo   The *Daily Beacon* asked me to be a part of the team covering Nancy's ascent from the UK. Local interest.

So amongst the wedding prep I am also following weather systems across the Himalayas and checking in with you.

Nancy   It was nice.

Theo   I was able to get exclusive quotes from Nancy by phone on the conditions and the team dynamics. Snaps of Everest.

Nancy   And I got to hear some Derbyshire vowels.

Amongst so much Français in the team.

Theo   And I'm also asking her to plan her speech.

'For the wedding, Nancy.'

Nancy   Yes.

Yes. How would you feel about some French philosophy?

There's this guy, René Daumaul, who wrote 'Mount Analogue'.

He was actually a –

Theo   French mountaineer, yes I know.

Nancy   Yes, but you might not know he

Theo   – died before it was finished,

Nancy   – so the book actually ends mid-sentence.

Is that how you'd like to go?

Mid –

Theo   Nance?

Nancy.

Nancy   You were meant to say sentence.

Theo   Sure.

And you're feeling confident. For making the ascent tomorrow?

Nancy   *Oui.*

Absolutement.

(*To the audience*.) On the expedition was a French mountaineer. I'd met him at Banff Mountain Film Festival. Jean-Pierre Brosse.

He was . . . very. Green. But charming.

We'd share champagne in my tent at Base Camp and gaze up at Everest. Trace the horizon on each other's backs.

Theo   Easy –

Nancy   and *have* each other's backs. Which is a great advantage.

And then when we're making our move. From Base Camp to Camp 1. Getting provisions sorted and deciding when we'll set off for the summit.

He says he can't wait to see me lit by the sunrise on Lhotse.

Pfffft.

Theo   She didn't tell me any of this.

Nancy   Lay in bed at Camp 2.

You can hear the jetstream roaring by Everest above.

Barely sleep.

Set off at 3am. Don't speak, make oxygen choices.

And we're ascending and ascending.

And then Jean-Pierre yells. Shrieks.

He's mis-stepped, and fell, a little.

Become caught in the fixed ropes on the Lhotse Face. And he's beginning to dislodge rocks. As he squirms. Rocks that cascade down below him. And narrowly miss the Canadian climbers.

He's panicking.

Which is a terrible oxygen choice.

We pause. And and untether him. Settle him a touch.

He's crying and we're still far far from the summit.

But he's struggling to breathe. Consistently.

He's reaching for his supplementary oxygen tanks in his bag. But we're still on the ascent.

And all of us. Wince a little.

So I. I just say it.

If you want to use your oxygen.

Why not go down to Base Camp and join the European team there.

You could leave us some of the kit from your bag, if you want to make your load lighter.

It's a team sport until it's not.

Theo   We were told the group had been successful.

Without supplementary oxygen, or a sherpa. It's monumental. Nancy's first mountain above 8,000 metres.

We receive a picture, for the article on the summit of Lhotse, Everest framed behind them. Perfect.

And then our sister website reports an interview with Jean-Pierre Brosse from Base Camp.

'She was cruel, and unsportsmanlike. Nancy Debenham.

She ended my dream of seeing the summit. And left me to descend the mountain alone. And heartbroken.

She's the worst kind of athlete.'

Nancy   The *worst kind of athlete.* Is not the title I was aiming for.

Theo   Our coverage becomes '*Scandal on the Mountain. Lovers' tiff almost costs lives!*'

I just did some basic copy. Some background, fact-checking.

It's not even my name on it.

(*To* **Nancy**.) Nancy, it wasn't my name on it.

Honestly, I was hardly in the office.

Between the venue and the florists and the rehearsal
dinner –

Nancy   I get back to England.

Get dropped by PeakKit.

Have a telling off from the French Ambassador to England.

And the English Ambassador to France.

And think this is enough. Actually.

Suffisamment.

Get back to Dad's.

Theo (*as* **Dad**)   Nancy, are you coming in the car with me
then tomorrow, duck?

Nancy   And I make a plan.

Theo   And on the day itself. Nancy *did* deliver. Rise to the
occasion.

Nancy   I did *a* speech.

Theo   It's just it was at a press conference in town. Not my
wedding.

Which called away at least three of the guests too. My
workmates. Far more empty chairs than I'd planned for.
When the MC said it was *time for the speeches, and would Nancy
like to ascend . . . the podium!*

Theo *looks around waiting.*

rather than let there be a silence.

It was Dad that ended up saving the day actually.

'I wondered if I could get your attention.

And I'm going to dare to speak on behalf of those that can't be here today.

Which if you knew my Rita, is a big ask. But I do know, we're very proud of you, Theodore. All of us.

And of you, Liam. Thank you for rescuing Theo from the places we can't reach.

Many, many years of joy. Is what I wish you. Up next, is mine and your mum's song. So.

I wonder if we might have a dance too, lad.'

'If I Could Turn Back Time' by Cher plays, **Theo** *dances by himself, recreating the moment briefly.* **Nancy** *attempts to speak over the music.*

Nancy   – and so I'd like to challenge the idea that I owed Jean-Pierre Brosse anything other than honesty. And I wonder why it was that he felt I would sugarcoat what was actually a decision to save his life. And the expedition. Was it because I'm a woman?

I don't see how being female should mean being predetermined to go easier on anyone.

I don't know what claim he feels he has to discredit my name.

But it is my name.

And *I* will be the only authority on what that means.

It is all I have.

Theo *leaves.*

Years pass.

Scene Twelve

Nancy   I'm twenty-eight.

I have three of the 8,000-metre mountains under my belt. Still Annapurna 1 to go though. Turns out it's not for the fainthearted.

I'm being driven across the Himalayas singing Madonna at the top of my lungs, in between base camps.

My ex has just left me because he was starting to wonder if I was only using him to help me carry my kit. Lhotse left a stain on my reputation.

But belting out 'Papa Don't Preach' in this light, burnt orange skies.

Fuck him.

FUCK HIMMMMMMMMMMMMMMM.

So this time, the Annapurna Circuit, ending with Annapurna 1.

About a third of climbers die on it.

Mum is counted in that figure too.

So just probability-wise. When I'm at base camp and there's three of us setting off in the same week. Letitia Rue. Maddie Sonali and me.

And we all say we want to do it solo. The air thins.

I'm here on a sponsorship the Alpine Mountaineering Trust called the Rarely Make History Fund.

We say we'll do some of the other peaks together, and then each do Annapurna 1.

It's brutal here, to be fair.

The first ascent was in 1950 – Maurice Herzog lost his gloves . . . and then his hands to frostbite whilst trekking.

The quickest route was a speedclimber. Twenty-eight hours.

Theo   I've become the type of customer they call in Aldi, a speed-packer.

The cashiers are always thrilled because it means you're keeping up with their pace.

Arms moving double-time in their thick fleeces.

We go in tandem.

Nancy   It's beautiful here. Annapurna 2.

We climb together.

And in the orange dome of our tents – like someone's halved a satsuma and jammed it on the mountain, we talk about the women who came before us, like Hilaree Nelson. Alison Hargreaves.

And they say they think Jean-Pierre Brosse was unfair to target you. That you have to look after yourself. And we talk a bit about Ueli Steck.

This incredible speedclimber.

And no one mentions how far he fell. And his wife left behind.

But the thought would bloom in my head like a fungus.

'is survived by . . .'

That's what it will say on my Wikipedia page. Still incredibly cringeworthy that I have a Wikipedia page. And survived by who?

Theo's mentioned.

He doesn't get a hyperlink, but his climbing the roof article gets a mention in the References section.

He's probably in his new place now.

Theo   Liam and I have bought a house, just the other side of Atterbury, not too far from Dad's.

And it has a bedroom. For the nursery.

Being able to prove you can be a foster parent is easier when you've been together as long as we have, Liam says.

I still feel like it's all happened quite suddenly.

How comfortable it all is.

I can drive straight in to Derby and then into the studios for work.

It's only local news coverage at the moment but it's been great to *see my town through other people's stories.*

Sometimes I drive the long way home just to see some hills.

And when people in shops find out I'm a journalist they say 'hey as long as you're sure it's off the record'.

And then eventually they ask 'how's your sister doing?'

And I say.

Yeah, I think she's fine.

Nancy   I order something for him on my phone. A gesture. Housewarming-wise. The phone signal can be surprisingly good at altitude.

I go to send a text too. *My brother, the homeowner.*

'How's the new place? You climbing up the walls yet?'

. . .

Don't send it.

He'll probably be busy.

Whatever his busy is.

Scene Thirteen

Theo   I've been going to yoga.

I'm not as strong as I used to be, but it's felt good, it's felt right waking my body up again.

You're not an athlete if you stop, are you?

You're just a fan. Or a has-been.

And if you used to be something really extraordinary. Roofboy.

What are you then? When you stop?

On the drive home, Siri reads out a text from our social worker saying 'Theodore, can your house be ready for a little boy who needs a home in the next few days? Xo Tina'.

I can't breathe a little.

I can't call Liam I don't know how to use my hands other than gripping the steering wheel and driving.

FUCKKKKKKKKKKKKKKKKKKKKKKKKKKKKKKK.

That's actually really big, actually huge, actually massive, monumental.

I get back to the house and there's a package on the doorstep.

Open it up.

It's a satsuma-coloured fleece.

With a note saying:

'Remember who you are, Simba,

Live in the orange.'

Cheek of it.

Scene Fourteen

Nancy *ascending a mountain ridge in Nepal – speaking into phone.*

Nancy   And I'm here! Made it!

To *the* top of Annapurna 1 at oh this is 26,500 feet and the view is extraordinary! Feel like I can probably see all of you! it's been a little bit scary climbing solo but it's nice having you guys on on here and the signal's incredible actually yeah.

Just an insane view, definitely worth it.

Makes you feel. Like you really exist. Rarely Make History Fund, I appreciate it.

She stops the Instagram story. She smiles. Looks around. Pauses.

I've made it.

And. Mum's up here. Out here. Somewhere. Close.

I call Theo.

'Hello?

Can you, can you hear me?'

Theo   Errr, yeah.

Nancy   Is it the signal –

Theo   No, it's just. I'm just in Aldi, can I call you back?

Nancy   Errm, not really.

Theo   Well hang on, let me go to a quieter section then, it's carnage on a Saturday. Sorry, I just really have to stock up on supplies, are you alright then – (*To a shopper.*) No, you move – (*back to* **Nancy**) whereabouts are you?

Nancy (*to audience*)   And then I hear him stop and smile as he realised where I must be, and all the space around me.

And he says

Theo   What elevation we talking?

Nancy   8,091 metres above sea level.

Just me, and the tops.

What are you doing?

Theo   Errm.

Food shop.

Annapurna 1. Fuck.

Nancy   It's big innit.

Theo   Awh I'm that pleased for you.

Nancy   Say it again.

Theo   Awh I'm that pleased for you.

Nancy   Cheers duck.

And I describe the final day and the weather conditions and I send him a picture.

And then he asks.

Theo   Weird question.

Can you tell Mum's been there?

A pause.

Nancy   Yeah she's around.

She feels near.

Theo   The ice field isn't it –

Nancy   No, Theo. I think she's just over the summit. With a hot chocolate. Waiting.

Theo   You send her my love won't you?

Nancy   Well you do it too then.

Theo   What do you mean?

Nancy   Well she's not just here is she?

Theo   I'm in the frozen food aisle of Aldi.

Nancy   Well she loved the cold.

If I yell 'Mum we love you', you have to do it too.

Promise.

Theo   What do you mean?

Nancy   No, Theo, promise you'll do it this time.

Theo   No Nancy –

Nancy   – you ready?

Both   MUM WE LOVE YOU!

Theo   – *Everyone is looking at me.*

Nancy   Worth it.

Theo   Yeah maybe.

Nancy   She can hear us.

Theo   Do you reckon?

Nancy   Yeah she's been with me.

When I've needed her.

Has she been with you?

Theo   Yeah. At. At the wedding. Sounds silly but. I really felt close to her.

It was a beautiful day actually.

But felt kinda wrong without you.

Nancy   Maybe it just felt wrong.

Right, I'll text you when I'm down shall I?

Theo   Nance. You can't just say that.

Like your opinion's worth shit anyway.

I am actually very happy down here. And we're going to foster!

And I hope you're happy up there on your own.

Did you hear that?

Nancy   I missed tha –

– Signal. I think it's on your end.

Theo   Everything's fine on my end.

I think it's you you should be worried about.

Nancy.

*****

(*To audience.*) It's the descents.

When people let down their guard.

And gravity's getting smug.

And all your careful planning and watchful footsteps feel less important because you've done the thing and you've got the adrenaline and you're so proud of yourself. But the mountain doesn't care. You're still just a guest, or really a trespasser. And trespassers get evicted.

They won't – she won't tell you that.

How many bodies there are up there. Still.

In positions you cannot reach, that have been swept down or where a serac, a column of glacial ice just breaks away and knocks you from your footing.

There are so many ways things can change that you absolutely cannot control.

There are –

Nancy (*to* **Theo**)   Alright Theo. I *am* still out here yaknow.

Theo   Yeah, you are, you're still out there anyway. Regardless.

He looks over at her.

Say something then.

He look back at the audience.

And I wonder if I jinxed it.

Because I didn't hear anything else from her.

I spent all of the day getting the house ready and and and fuck where sells nightlights and plastic cutlery and beanbag chairs?

And my heartbeat told me 'not good not good not good not good not good'.

And I went to yoga and I got home and there was a lady on my doorstep. And she looked worried.

Sam Randall   Have you not heard?

Theo   What?

Sam Randall   Nancy's not made contact with Base Camp today.

And one of the other climbers making an attempt in the same timeframe has been swept off in an avalanche.

Letitia Rue.

I've just come from her parents'.

Theo   Who are you?

Sam Randall   I just thought it was important you knew.

I'm very keen you get to tell your story. Did you get to speak to her?

Did she say anything you think would have been potentially suspect?

Theo   You're Sam Randall aren't you?

Sam Randall   It's lovely to see you so well, Theo.

Theo   Sam, can you get the fuck off my drive?

Sam Randall   Sorry.

Theo   This is how you fucking tell someone their sister's missing?

BAD CONDUCT.

(*To audience.*) I check every newsapp I could, every post, every scrap of information and there are pictures of Mum and Nancy at every possible opportunity, these dots that every fucking news site was so pleased to have joined up.

(*To audience.*) And I went straight to Dad's.

Nancy (*as* **Dad**)   Oh, was I expecting you?

I didn't think you'd want dinner, thought it was tomorrow you were working late?

Oh no, you might have another mouth by then, right?

Is that why you've come over in a tizz is it?

It's a mammoth thing what's happening. But I understand it, lad. I do.

I can make you summet.

Theo   Dad, Nancy's not reported back to base.

A pause.

Nancy (*as* **Dad**)   Oh. Is that so?

Theo   Sam Randall told me.

Nancy (*as* **Dad**)   Sam Randall?

You met Sam Randall?

. . .

Why?

Theo   She was at my door.

Nancy (*as* **Dad**)   I can't believe she's still writing.

Theo   Dad?!

Would you listen?

Nancy's out there and they can't track her.

Nancy (*as* **Dad**)   I did hear you.

And I am.

Very sorry this has happened.

Very deeply sorry this has happened Theo.

That's all I can say about it.

Theo   There's a mission. There'll be a mission, I'll call the embassy. I'll.

So what are we doing about it?

Nancy (*as* **Dad**)   Well I can't do anything 'bout it can I?

Look at me!

Theo, Nancy is her own woman.

She is smart.

And capable.

Theo   Yeah and that mountain is the deadliest mountain, Dad.

The deadliest.

The deadliest.

And we let her do it, let her just do it.

You were talking to her.

You should have stopped her.

Nancy (*as* **Dad**)   Theodore, what are you trying to do to me?

I'm an old man.

Look at me.

I gave up chasing you both, years ago.

You're meant to take care of her for me.

Theo   Well. I'm not giving up on her.

Nancy (*as* **Dad**)   No one's giving up on her.

Theo   You're not doing fucking anything.

Nancy (*as* **Dad**)   Listen.

I am the most broken-hearted man, Theo.

You've got more left in your tank than I do.

Nancy *leaves*.

Theo   WELL I'LL GO THEN.

Scene Fifteen

Theo   bahhhhHHHHHHHHHHHHHHHHHHH.

I come home and pack in a fury.

Liam can't really speak to me, I don't know what to tell him that's not

'I need to know where she is.'

He says this will be a real risk to our place on the list.

That George didn't make a choice to be in the position he's in, but Nancy did.

Says well where will you sleep what will you do I can't come with you we can't afford this.

I buy a ticket to Kathmandu Airport.

I say sorry. I think.

Twelve hours. Make it make sense with work, say whatever they need to hear.

I might have quit.

I don't think so.

I sit on the plane.

And it's not good not good not good not good not good not good.

If it's been the last –

If I could ever –

If I knew what –

If I could tell her –

If Mum hadn't –

If Mum hadn't –

And her sponsors – The phone signal –

If I'd just turned around and looked at her a bit more just
looked at her following me trusting me listening to me
copying me if I'd been more generous and swallowed my
pride if I'd made her come to dinner with Liam involved her
with ice cream told her I was going to be a dad with my
whole chest and I if I'd kept climbing if I'd gone out there
with her If I could turn back time If I could find a way I'd
take back those words that have hurt you

*Maybe 'If I Could Turn Back Time' by Cher overtakes him briefly
as he sits paralysed.*

*****

I touch down.

And it's chaos, mayhem. Airport. Traffic.

'Would you do an interview?'

They've brought her off the mountain.

It took three days to track where she would have been given
how hard the winds were.

They could see the orange of her tent.

That's how they knew it was her, the orange of her tent.

They say 'do I want to see her do you want to see her sir.'

I say 'I think so.'

'I've come all this way.'

'It makes sense you'd want to see her.'

Scene Sixteen

Theo *enters the hospital room, in a huge climbing coat and rucksack.*

Nancy   Well take your coat off or you won't feel 'benefit.

Theo   You.

Nancy   Tadah!

You can look pleased to see me.

Do you want a Lotus biscuit? Please take some I've got twelve.

They keep bringing them out and they get clogged in my teeth.

Theo   No.

Where are they?

No.

Nancy   They'll bring more when they bring out the sad coffee.

You can sit down if – you want.

Theo   – They said your tent was millimetres from a crevasse.

Nancy   It was.

Theo   Three days.

Nancy   I did a lot of singing to myself.

A lot of Madonna –

Theo   – How could you be so stupid?

Nancy   Whoa.

Theo   – So fucking stupid selfish careless narrow-minded.

Nancy   – *Theo* I'm in actual pain here, really not not in a place to receive this kind of –

Theo   – PIGheaded.

Nancy   – PIGheaded?

Theo   Yeah, you heard.

Nancy   That is.

So mean.

Theo   I mean it.

I mean it.

Do you know how close you were to dying?

Irretrievably.

Nancy   I'm pretty sure all deaths are irretrievable.

Theo   No. You stop that now.

We are not having fun now.

Liam was like, oh go easy on her, she's in shock, she's in pain –

Nancy   – he's right –

Theo   You're in your fucking element.

The hero returned.

We nearly lost you.

Properly.

Where do you want to be buried?

Feels like the kind of thing me and Dad ought to know nowadays?

Am I reading a poem?

Am I scattering your ashes at whichever Base Camp or would Kinder Scout be okay?

Nancy   Errm.

Depends if you'd be able to retrieve me I guess.

Theo   Listen to yourself.

Nancy   Listen to *YOURSELF.*

What exactly are you angry for?

I'm shattered.

I'm on so many painkillers I drooled for an hour and thought there'd been a leak in the roof.

My hip is fucked.

My shoulder blade is in two bits.

I'm here.

Somehow you've managed to just make it all about you so far.

You just had to get a flight and colour-coordinate your fucking ski jacket, Roofboy.

SIT DOWN.

And have a biscuit.

He does.

Theo   It was a long flight. Long-haul flight.

I thought you'd died.

I thought you'd died this time.

Nancy   I'm sorry.

. . .

Theo   Did you realise you'd packed too much kit – you were far heavier than you needed to be?

Nancy   Awh yaknow what Theo, do you wanna piss off and come back in and do this again a bit better please?

Really upset now.

. . .

Theo   Are we hugging?

Nancy   Not if you don't mean it, your hugs are so limp.

Theo   I am glad to see you.

Nancy   Why is that so hard for you to say?

Theo   There's a lot going on.

Nancy   There's not, it's so boring here.

It's gonna be a few weeks apparently.

And then physio.

And then scans and things.

God that mountain's beautiful though.

I would do it again.

Maybe.

You should've seen it.

Theo   I WAS ABOUT TO.

It was all taking so long.

I bought all this stuff.

Nancy   They wouldn't have let you up the mountain.

Theo, *they would not have let you up the mountain, would they?*

You're not good enough.

Theo   Right.

He goes to pick up his stuff.

Nancy   *ANYMORE.*

Theo   I had a journalist pass.

Nancy   You were going to cover my disappearance?

Theo   Well they weren't doing it right. *Disappearance.*

They kept talking about Mum instead of you.

Nancy   Oh.

. . .

Which photo did they use?

Her in the –

Both   – blue jacket with us in Wales.

Theo   Headline was:

'Fatefully reunited on Annapurna 1'

Nancy   No.

Theo   Sam Randall came to find me.

Nancy   Urgh. What was she like?

Theo   Strange.

Fuck ass bob though.

Nancy   No.

Theo   Yeah really.

People were calling it a suicide mission, Nancy.

Nancy   Well it wasn't.

Theo, it wasn't.

Theodore.

Theo   Just a very dangerous time of year to go.

And solo.

And unaided, without supplementary oxygen.

And quickly.

Nancy   – For the funding, Theo.

All had to be firsts didn't it?

And it won't even count as a successful attempt will it, because I got helicoptered down.

Theo   I can't cope with this.

I've got things to get back to.

Nancy   What?

Theo   I have a family now.

Nancy   Liam isn't your family, Liam's a moss you've accumulated from staying still.

Theo   Yes he fucking is. My family.

And yours now (*shows the ring*)

And we're going to foster a little boy.

Nancy   What?

Theo   I did tell you on the phone.

Nancy   No you didn't.

Theo   Yes. Yes. Your signal was bad.

You should've got down as soon as the signal got bad by the way.

Nancy   You were in Aldi, didn't even think to leave Aldi to try and speak to me clearer.

Theo   I was surprised to hear from you.

Nancy   Well congratulations.

Theo.

. . .

Theo congratulations.

Theo   Little four-year-old boy, we're we're going to foster and see how long he needs us for.

He's called George.

Nancy   That's huge.

Theo   It is a bit.

Nancy   You feeling alright about it?

Theo   Think so.

Nancy   . . .

Well.

. . .

Awh I'm that pleased for you.

Theo   Yeah.

Yeah thanks.

Say it again.

Nancy   I'm that pleased for you.

. . .

Theo.

Theo   Yes.

Nancy   Can you come closer?

Theo   Yes.

You're not gonna burp are you?

Nancy   No.

Theo   Wait, you're not dying are you?

Nancy   NO.

Theo   You're not going to say something profound and just leave me here in urban Nepal.

Nancy   No.

I.

I have something to tell you.

Theo   Well I do too but I thought it was a given.

Like I can say it if you want me too, I just thought it was a given.

Nancy   No it's probably not that.

Theo   Well let's say it together then and then it's less cringey.

Nancy   No, Theo it's.

Theo   3, 2, 1.

– I love you.

Nancy   – I'm pregnant.

I love *YOU!*

Theo   What?

Nancy   Right?!

Bit mad.

Theo   This is really serious.

(*More serious.*) and are you still?

Nancy   Yep. They said it's still there so.

Theo   Did you know?

Nancy   I had an inkling.

Theo   How?

Nancy   I just felt heavier.

Was eating more.

Crying more.

Didn't have periods.

Missed you.

Theo   Who's the dad?

Nancy   Oh fuck I ought to tell the dad.

Theo   Who *is* the dad?

Is it Jean-Pierre Brosse? Rodrigo Hernandez?

Is it sports personality Eli Fletcher?

Is it Robert Bollington?

Nancy   Have you got a list? Jesus Christ.

Theo   I talk to all your exes.

Nancy   Why?

Theo   In case you die.

I don't want to have to remember you alone.

I need some teammates.

Nancy   Christ, you've given this some thought.

Hey.

I'm here, aren't I?

And anyway, you'd be much better at living without me, than I would be without you.

Theo   You mustn't think that.

You don't honestly think that do you?

You're going to be a mum.

How far along?

Nancy   Like three months.

Theo   Do you want to keep it?

Nancy   I think so.

Well yaknow.

The baby really wanted to live didn't it?

Survived an avalanche.

Must be made of bungee cord or something.

Theo   Will you be taking some time off?

Nancy   I AM TAKING SOME TIME OFF.

Theo   You're bedbound. That's not the same.

Nancy   Alright you're coming in really hot again. They're gonna come in here and really tell you off if you keep having a go at me. My monitors.

Theo   You look like a grandparent from a Roald Dahl book.

Come stay with us when you come home.

Or Dad's.

I can help.

Nancy   Well I'll need something of my own in the long run.

Theo   Course.

Nancy   And then when I start going out again, I'd make sure your room was done up to stay yeah.

Theo   Hang on. What?

Wait, you honestly think you'll still climb?

Nancy how?

How can you think that?

Nancy   Well I'd be out of action for a bit.

But this is what I'm for.

Theo   You're not gonna be there for your own baby?

Nancy   YOU came out here, didn't you? Isn't George meant to be with you now?

Theo   But that's a bit different isn't it?

Nancy   Is it? Sounds like that child really needs support and you scarpered.

Theo   I'm here for you!

Nancy   Clearly!

I wouldn't be an absent mother. I'd be providing at least.

Like Mum did.

Theo   She couldn't be any more absent, Nance, she died.

And she wasn't a saint, Nancy.

She was selfish and absent and and and detached. From us.

Nancy   All this time obsessing over her, and *that's* your takeaway?

She'd fly home whenever she could if you got sick. *That's* in the diaries.

She was torn from us. She wasn't heartless.

Theo   Just a bad bad world out there that she walked straight into.

Nancy   She was an *expert* at what she did. Most people just sleepwalk through their life.

And I can't protect mine from everything either anyway. Or you.

Theo   You can at least try? Nancy.

Bare minimum is to try and stay off a mountain for them.

Nancy   Statistically you're more likely to die in a police car chase than on a mountain climb.

And I've seen you drive a Punto.

Theo   If I die –

Nancy   Shut up, I was joking you won't –

Theo   I could. *I will.*

Who looks after my kid?

Nancy   Liam.

Theo   Well what if I wanted it to be you! What if I want you to be in its life?

Nancy   Do you?

Theo   Yes.

Nancy   Then why didn't you reach out?

Theo   I'm here aren't I?

Nancy   This whole time though.

Theo   You kept going off –

Nancy   To do this!

And you've held it against me. No, I can't do taxes properly can't clean an oven don't know spaghetti recipes.

I just know this.

Theo   You're much more capable than you make out.

Nancy   I'm just figuring it out.

Theo   Nancy you're unstoppable.

An avalanche couldn't do it.

(*He thinks.*) Two avalanches.

You were only eight.

And I'm so sorry for you.

Because yes actually, Mum *was* so good, Nancy. And you got so much less of her than me, and look what you've managed to do with it!

The the parenting stuff.

We can figure that out together can't we?

We can just sort of guess.

And I'll have you, and you'll have me. That's not nothing, that's huge.

Nancy   But it costs me. It costs me everything.

To give up.

I don't want them to think that their only paths are the signposted ones yaknow.

Because those weren't working for us were they?

We needed big.

To look at the feeling and put a hand to it.

And to scale it.

When the world was telling us how tragic it was to follow in her footsteps.

But they're such brilliant footsteps, Theo.

Who couldn't follow?

And and when it's right I will tell my little one.

Because we never got told did we?

They never prepared us that one time she might not come back.

Difference is, I'd tell them, even if it would be really hard.

Really fucking hard.

Fuck.

How do you tell them that?

And still go.

A pause.

I can't do it then can I, I can't have the kid or I have to stop.

I'll just have to. Stop.

Theo   Would that be so bad?

Move into a cul-de-sac.

Nancy   Mhmm.

Just do that forever.

Learn some spaghetti recipes.

Get Tupperware.

Go parents' evening.

Theo   Have nights in.

Bonfire Nights. Sparklers.

Collecting shells on beaches.

Nancy   Get an office job.

Take annual leave.

Spend time with them. Walks around Froggatt. Saturdays. Sundays.

Have a pension. Save for a pension. Take each day as it is.

And be still. And settled. And wait it out.

. . .

Do you wanna know how big it is right now?

Theo   The baby? I dunno. Little. Very little.

Nancy   A satsuma.

Theo   That's. That's a good orange that.

Theo *smiles.* **Nancy** *still looks uncertain. She puts a hand on her stomach.*

Theo   It is, isn't it? It's second prize to you. To be a mum and not also this.

. . . Then please don't choose that.

Nancy   Am I broken? That that's not enough?

Theo   No.

Nancy   I can't *just* do that. I can't.

I don't want to lose you ever.

But I can't give this up. If it's what I'm for.

I'm sorry I missed the wedding.

I'll try. A bit harder. To show up.

Would you help me?

Theo   Well.

It was quite exciting doing a long-haul flight. I've. Never done that.

We could visit you. Keep an eye on you.

I'm going to be new to it too, Nance.

Nancy   You'll have had a headstart though.

With George.

Theo   You'll catch up.

. . .

At least wait until you know they're old enough to get through it.

Nancy   We have to promise not to die until we know they can get through it?

I don't think we can promise that.

Theo   Say it with me and then it's true.

It's true for us.

Nancy   What are we promising then?

Theo   To keep living.

Nancy   To keep living.

Theo   And to tell them the worst could happen.

Nancy   And tell them the worst could happen.

Theo   It can't just be that.

Nancy   Well when they know that. At least.

At least they'll know they've got to really live

. . .

Theo   How do we tell them then?

Nancy   Errrm.

When the time's right.

When we can tell that the time's right.

We sit them down.

And then.

And then we let them know about Mum. And us. And how she *lived*.

Theo   How we *lived*.

Nancy   We tell them together.

End.